THOU SHALT DECREE AND DELCARE

**Thou Shall Decree A Thing, And It
Shall Be Established Unto Thee.
— Job 22:28**

Walking With An Established Heart

WRITTEN BY
CORRINE S. PAYNE

*Through decreeing a thing, your heart will
become established in the word of faith.*

Thou Shall Decree a Thing, Job 22:28: Walking With An Established Heart

Trilogy Christian Publishers A Wholly Owned Subsidiary of Trinity Broadcasting Network
2442 Michelle Drive Tustin, CA 92780

Manufactured in the United States of America
10 9 8 7 6 5 4 3 2 1
Library of Congress Cataloging-in-Publication Data is available.
ISBN: 978-1-63769-436-7
E-ISBN: 978-1-63769-437-4

2

Acknowledgment

I thank God and the Holy Spirit for their inspiration in writing this book. I would get inspirational thoughts from the Holy Spirit as I was writing and found them in the Word. Much thanks go to our daughter, Demetra Payne, and son, Henry J. Payne, for working and helping me with my computer set up. They taught me the different icons to work with on the computer, which I wasn't familiar with. I am very grateful for my husband, who always inspires, encourages, and prays for me and the success of my book.

THOU SHALL DECREE A
THING AND IT SHALL
BE ESTABLISHED UNTO
THEE: AND

THE LIGHT SHALL
SHINE UPON THOU
WAYS.

—JOB 22:28

TABLE OF
CONTENTS

PREFACE

This manuscript was born in 2014 on my home computer. Afterward, the computer went out, I put it in the shop for a period of time. When I picked it up out of the shop and brought it home, and connected it, there was a loud noise like something was broken or loose, and I said I would return it later. I had a feeling it would cost more money than I had in my account. So, I just let it sat until this year, 2021. I do believe that God orchestrates things to happen at his perfect timing. Therefore, I said to myself, I am taken this computer to the shop so I can get my book ready for publishing. This book will bless the readers as they read with an open mind because it was inspired by the Holy Spirit, and when I read it on my computer? I said wow! to my husband. This book will help you to become established in the word of faith as you believe, receive, and apply it to your life. As you meditate on the scriptures, they will empower you and give insight into your life.

INTRODUCTION

God's Word is more than enough to meet every challenge we are faced with in life. His Word is a living and powerful word which no foe can withstand. John 1:1-4 says, "in the beginning, was the Word, and the Word was with God, and the Word was God." The same was in the beginning with God. All things were made by Him and without Him was not anything made that was made. In Him was life, and the life was the light of men. The Word was in the beginning in creation; God spoke and brought everything into existence by His words. He demonstrated how powerful and profound His Word is when He made the universe and created man by His spoken Word. The Word is light and will give life to those who will take it at face value; it shines out in the life of the believer to give light to those who are sitting in darkness. It is a lamp to your feet and a light unto your path; it will keep you from stumbling and falling if you will adhere and obey it. It says in Hebrew 4:12, "for the word of the Lord is quick, and powerful, and sharper than any two-edged sword, piercing even to the dividing asunder of soul and spirit and of the joints and marrow, and is a discerner of the thoughts and intents of the heart." The Word of God will give you life on the inside and cause others to see it on the outside because it is the ZOE kind of life. It is so powerful you can feel it working on the inside when you receive and live it out. Proverb 4: 22 says, God's words are life unto those that find them and health to all their flesh. The words of God will heal you

11

and make you whole when it is applied to your life. God's Word is activated when you speak it out of your mouth and believe it in your heart. It is the word of faith, which we are saved and delivered by. It keeps us protected and shields us from the fiery darts of the enemy. It is a discerner of the thought and intent of the heart; it knows what you are thinking and how to captivate the thoughts of your mind and bring peace when there is turmoil. God's Word is medicine to our flesh; it will heal the soul and body; it healed my mind on several occasions. I labor in the Word, putting it before my eyes and in my heart, taking it like medicine twice a day and sometimes three times a day, believing it, standing on it, and declaring it until it raised me up from weakness to strength. You see, God upholds everything by the words of His power, and there is nothing that His Word cannot accomplish if we believe. His words are true and hold truth; whatever the Bible says it will do, it will. I am a firm believer of the Word. I have experienced it in my life, and seen it work in my family lives, and invite you to receive the Word of life which is able to save you and give you an inheritance.

Roman 10:8-9 put it this way, "but what saith it? He asked a question, the word is nigh thee, even in thy mouth and in thy heart; that is the word of faith, which we preach; that if thou shalt confess with thou mouth the Lord Jesus, and believe in thine heart that God hath raised him from the dead thou shall be saved. For with the heart man believe unto righteousness, and with the mouth, confession is made unto salvation." You see, the Word we preached gives life when it is received by faith and will save you. Salvation is a gift that we can't work for or achieve on our own; it is by grace through faith that we are saved, healed, and delivered, and set free.

Submitting to God's Word is essential to the growth of your faith: your love for Him will always tell the story because He said in His Word if you love me, keep my commandments, and that requires a decision of obedience on your part and implementation.

If you want to prosper from within, choose God's Word daily above all else and see it began to change your life and circumstances; 3 John 2 put it like this; "beloved, I wish above all things that thou mayest prosper and be in health even as thou soul prosper." What was he saying? Giving God's Word first place will cause you to prosper in every area of your life. Amen!

GIVE GOD'S WORD FIRST PLACE

I decree and declare that "God's Word is quick and powerful and sharper than any two-edged sword, piercing even to the dividing asunder of soul and spirit, and of the joints and marrow, and is a discerner of the thoughts and intents of the heart" (Hebrews 4:12).

PRACTICAL APPLICATION

According to Hebrew 4:12, an Individual must take the Word of God by faith and pray over their body and circumstances, asking God for wisdom and insight on what to do. Be patient and wait on God to answer, stay consistent, in the Word, don't allow doubt to enter into your heart. The Word will discern your thoughts and the motive of your heart. Meaning it knows what you are thinking, what you are going to do before you do it. It will speak to you on the inside and tell you what to do; most of the time, if we don't know the voice of the Lord through His Word, we will ignore it. The Holy Spirit is the voice to God's Word, and He is going to speak in line with that Word, which is why we are to feed upon it; it is food for the spiritual man, just like physical food is for the body. The Word of God will quicken you, making you alive on the inside. It will give you the power to stand when you are going through your test and trials. Maybe you are going through a situation right now and not sure what to do; be led by the Holy Spirit, and He will show you what to do. We do not move until God confirmed it through prayer and His Word; the victory always lies in what God tells you to do, followed by your obedience.

***

I DECREE AND DECLARE the Bible says, "as many as received Him, to them gave He, power to become the sons of God, even to them that believe upon his name" (John 1:12).

PRACTICAL APPLICATION

You are a son/daughter of God, and He has given you the Holy Spirit: which is your power source. He's inside you, and as you feed on the Word and receive it, you will grow in the Lord with confidence and assurance. You will become stronger in faith, your prayer life will deepen, and you won't be easily offended, and others will see the light inside you because you are not the same; you are a child of God and believe upon His name. A change took place in your life, and you and others will see the newness in you.

***

I DECREE AND DECLARE, "in him was Life: In him was life; and the life was the light of men..." (John 1:4)

16

PRACTICAL APPLICATION

John, who was one of the apostles, writes, "in Jesus Christ we have life;" idol can't give life, only God can. And the life that's in Him is in us; light represents life, and it illuminates, and it will dispel darkness; as we yield our spirit to Christ and obey His Word, we will become brighter as we change from glory to glory and faith to faith. And others will begin to identify with your light.

***

I DECREE AND DECLARE, "in the beginning was the word, and the word was with God, and the word was God. The same was in the beginning with God" (John 1:1-2).

PRACTICAL APPLICATION

There is life in the Word of God. We can believe it or not. The word spoken brought everything into existence in creation. God said, "let there be light, and it was so." The angel Gabriel spoke to Mary and said, she was to have the promise child, she replied, be it unto me according to thou word.

***

I DECREE AND DECLARE the Bible says, "my son, attend to my words incline thine ears to my sayings let them not depart from thine eyes; keep them in the midst of thine heart, for they are life unto those that find them, and health to all their flesh" (Proverb 4:20-22).

17

THOU SHALT DECREE AND DELCARE

PRACTICAL APPLICATION

Keeping the Word before your eyes, confessing it over your body and situation, will bring healing, health, and deliverance in your life. This works, I've used it in my own life, and the Word works. I was sick, and I tookGod's Word just as the Scripture said and kept it before my eyes, confessing it every day, and it brought healing to my flesh. Being consistent is the key.

FAITH

I DECREE AND DECLARE, "for we walk by faith and not by sight" (2 Corinthians 5:7).

PRACTICAL APPLICATION

The Bible teaches us if we are going to receive anything from God, it's through faith and patience that we inherit the promises. Hebrews 11:6 for without faith, it is impossible to please God: We must believe the Word, receive it, and obey it, and apply it. We must believe He is a rewarder of them who diligently seek Him.

***

I DECREE AND DECLARE, "for whatsoever is born of God overcomes the world: and this is the victory that overcomes the world even our faith" (1 John 5:4).

PRACTICAL APPLICATION

Since we have been born again of God's Spirit, we have His nature, and we are overcomers, and as we feed on the Word and apply it daily and not yield to our flesh and the temptation of the world, we can live a life of victory.

***

I DECREE AND DECLARE, "Now faith is the substance of things hope for, and the evidence of things not seen" (Hebrews 11:1).

PRACTICAL APPLICATION

Faith is a substance, just as the brick material to build a house and ingredient to a cake; it is what makes things work. When we talk about faith as a substance, we are speaking of the Word of God. It is what causes our faith to grow and excel and bring things to pass in our lives. Faith comes when we hear the Word and keep hearing it. It's seeded in the heart and produces fruits of righteousness.

***

I DECREE AND DECLARE, "He staggered not at the promises of God through unbelief; but was strong in faith, giving glory to God; and being fully persuaded that, what he had promised, he was able also to perform" (Roman 4:20-21).

PRACTICAL APPLICATION

We do not have to stagger at the promises of God like a drunken man who staggers when he has had too much alcohol. We can be sober-minded through faith, believing what the Word of God says, giving praise and honor to God, and what He has said He would bring it to pass in our lives if we don't cave in and quit.

***

I DECREE AND DECLARE, "Trust in the Lord with all thine heart; and lean not to thine own understanding. In all thou ways acknowledge him, and he shall direct thy paths" (Proverb 3:5-6).

20

PRACTICAL APPLICATION

This should be one of every Christian confession each day, trusting in God, not self, not money, nor fame or fortune, but in the living Word of God. We should not lean to what we think, or how we feel, or by our reasoning, but in God's wisdom. We should come to Him and petition Him, what we should do, for He has promised to give us direction. When we become anxious, fearful, and impatient and take matters into our own hands, we forfeit God's plans.

***

I DECREE AND DECLARE, "and the prayer of faith shall save the sick, and the Lord shall raise him up; and if he hath committed sins, they shall be forgiven him" (James 5:15).

PRACTICAL APPLICATION

James tells us that the prayer of faith will save the sick: He is saying, when a person is sick and call for the elders of the church and they anoint him with oil and pray the prayer of faith over him, he will be healed and raised up again; and his sins are forgiven, because of his faith and obedience to the Word. It works!

***

I DECREE AND DECLARE "that the communication of thy faith may become effectual by the acknowledging of every good thing which is in you in Christ Jesus" (Philemon 1:6).

PRACTICAL APPLICATION

As we acknowledge every good thing which is in us,
that Christ has done through the finished work of Calvary,
our faith becomes effectual to our spirit, soul, and body,
and it will become evident in our lives as we appropriate
the Word.

***

I DECREE AND DECLARE, "But without faith, it is
impossible to please him: for he that cometh to God must
believe that he is, and that he is a rewarder of them that
diligently seek him" (Hebrews 11:6).

PRACTICAL APPLICATION

Believing is essential to salvation, healing, deliverance,
prosperity, and all our victories in Christ. So, therefore,
we cannot doubt because it is all these things that make up
your faith.

My Body Is the Temple of the Holy Spirit

I DECREE AND DECLARE: "What? Know ye not that your body is the temple of the Holy Ghost which is in you, which ye have of God, and ye are not your own? for ye are bought with a price: therefore, glorify God in your body, and in your spirit, which are God's." (1 Corinthians 6:19-20)

Practical Application

When our spirit is born again, we become the possession of God; we no longer belong to ourselves. He purchased us with His own blood on the cross and gave us Himself, that's why Paul tells us in Roman 12:1-2, to present our bodies a living Sacrifice, Holy and acceptable unto God, which is our motive for worship, but we go around acting as if we belong to ourselves, instead of God. We become self-sufficient in our own strength instead of His. The reason being, we have not surrendered to the Lordship of Jesus Christ. He continues to wait and love us until we commit our lives fully to Him.

***

I DECREE AND DECLARE, "for in him dwelleth all the fulness of the Godhead bodily. And ye are complete in him, which is the head of all principality and power" (Colossians 2:9-10).

THOU SHALT DECREE AND DELCARE

PRACTICAL APPLICATION

Colossians 1:27 tells us that Christ is in us the hope of glory, and we are in Him, which is the head of the church, and we are His body; therefore, we are whole in Him. We are winners; because we have all that we need in us, we have the Father, Son, and the Holy Spirit through the Word of God, which makes us complete in Him.

EMPOWERED BY THE HOLY SPIRIT

I DECREE AND DECLARE: "but ye shall receive power, after that the Holy Ghost is come upon you: and ye shall be a witness unto me both in Jerusalem, and in all Judea, and in Samaria, and unto the uttermost part of the earth" (Act 1:8).

PRACTICAL APPLICATION

In Scripture, every believer that is born again received the Spirit of God, but there is a Baptism of the Holy Ghost that causes a person to live in power and not defeat, to speak with other tongues, cast out devils, lay hands on the sick as he/she presses into Him (Holy Ghost) He is the one who equipped the believer with power to be a witness, and do the work of the ministry without being fearful or afraid. Our Jerusalem, Judea, and Samaria can be wherever we live because many Christian do not get a chance to go abroad preaching the Gospel to other nations, and whosoever God places in your path and send to you, you should be a witness for him.

***

I DECREE AND DECLARE, "For as many are led by the Spirit of God, they are the sons of God" (Roman 8:14).

Practical Application

To be led by the Spirit of God requires you to listen and pay attention to what He is saying. Then obey and apply His Word. You cannot be led by His Spirit if you are in disobedience; it doesn't work that way, even though you have been born again. Just like you require obedience of your own children. Many people think they can do anything and everything and still be led by God; they are self-deceived. James 1: 22 says, be a doer of the Word, and not hearer only deceiving your own selves. Yes, we are children of God, but we must do our part if we desire to live in victory.

***

I DECREE AND DECLARE, "The Spirit himself beareth witness with our spirit, that we are the children of God" (Roman 8:16).

Practical Application

The anointing will bear witness with your human spirit when you are in line with God's will for your life. He will speak to you inwardly concerning God's plans for you to follow. As you yield to His leadership, He will continue to lead and guide you into all truth.

***

I DECREE AND DECLARE, "but if the Spirit of him that raised up Jesus from the dead dwelled in you, he that raised up Christ from the dead shall also quicken your mortal bodies by his Spirit that dwelleth in you" (Roman 8:11).

26

Practical Application

The Spirit that raised Jesus from the dead is the same Spirit that empowers, quickens, and equipped us for ministry. When you read the Scriptures, you will find there is one Spirit, and He has many functions that He performs in the lives of the believers. When He quickens a person, it feels like a piecing of the soul, which makes alive and energizes you on the inside, causing you to receive and hear God's Word more clearly.

***

I DECREE AND DECLARE, "likewise the Spirit also helpeth our infirmities: for we know not what to pray for as we ought: but the Spirit himself makes intercession for us with groaning which cannot be uttered: and he that searched the hearts knoweth what is the mind of the spirit, because he maketh intercession for the saints according to the will of God. and we know that all things work together for good, to them that love God, to them who are the called according to his purpose." (Roman 8:26-28)

Practical Application

When I was sick last year, I stood on this Scripture, I decree and declared it over my body, that the Holy Spirit would make intercession for me with groaning which cannot be utter, I was praying in my prayer language at different times, and He was helping me by praying through me what I needed to be prayed. I was weak; no appetite wasn't sleeping, medicine didn't seem to work, I was in a condition only God could help. Trying to work on a job with no strength is hard; I had to sit down most of the time. During this period of my life, when it seems like I couldn't go any further, the power of God came on my body, in His anointing, strengthen and energized me, I worked the entire day strengthened and healed in His name, and because of Him interceding through me, I was able to reap the benefits. God is an awesome God!

Wisdom

I DECREE AND DECLARE, "wisdom is the principal thing; therefore, get wisdom: and with all thy getting get understanding" (Proverb, 4:7).

Practical Application

Wisdom is insight, which comes from God's Word. Just as Solomon gave his son instruction, we also give our children instruction, telling them to pay attention and get a clear understanding of what we are saying.

***

I DECREE AND DECLARE, "My son, attend unto wisdom, and bow thy ear to understanding: that thy mayest regard discretion, and that thou lips may keep knowledge" (Proverb 5:1-2).

Practical Application

Solomon is saying give your attention wholly to wisdom, and listen for the Holy Spirit to give you clarity of understanding, that you may know justice or what is right, and your lips may speak knowledge, for out of the abundance (fullness) of the heart the mouth speaks.

***

I DECREE AND DECLARE, "Hear; for I will speak of excellent things; and the opening of thy lips shall be right things" (Proverb 8:6).

PRACTICAL APPLICATION

As we apply the Word of God, which is His wisdom, we will speak of excellent things. God's wisdom will always excel over worldly knowledge which comes from man. But excellent things come from God.

***

I DECREE AND DECLARE, "wisdom dwell with prudence, and find out knowledge of witty inventions" (Proverb 8:12).

PRACTICAL APPLICATION

A child of God has everything he needs on the inside of him to be victorious; he has to take the initiative to appropriate it by faith. Because wisdom dwells within the believer and gives knowledge (a knowing or insight on what to do), you can be walking along or doing something, and a great idea can come into your human spirit, you may ask yourself, where did that come from? You may have been praying about something in the Spirit, and it's been revealed; if you act on that idea, it can be the witty invention, or maybe it's one word which Scripture gives that can alter your life forever and bring you into your wealthy place.

***

I DECREE AND DECLARE, "the fear of the Lord is to hate evil: pride, and arrogance, and the evil way, and the froward mouth, do I hate" (Proverb 8:13).

PRACTICAL APPLICATION

To reverence means to honor and respect God in our daily walk of life, we are to love what he loves and hate what he hates. All evils ways and wrong doing are tools of the devil; he uses them against the believers every day. We must be on guard and watch out for his entrapment and temptation and stand against them with righteousness in our walk with God. It is so easy to fall into a snare when everything is going smoothly, you can get caught up in the pride of life. We must remind ourselves continually that we are the heirs of God and made stewards over our assignment. And our attitude should be one of humility and not pride or arrogance. The forward mouth is perverse lips, it will say one thing and do another, and these things ought not to be, for the Bible teaches us to speak the truth in our hearts.

***

I DECREE AND DECLARE, "Through wisdom is an house builded; and by understanding it is established: and by knowledge shall the chambers be filled with all precious and pleasant riches" (Proverbs 24:3-4).

PRACTICAL APPLICATION

First, you must go to God in prayer, asking Him to bless you with a home if you don't have one. Afterward, release your faith for the revelation of His wisdom to know how to design your home. When you act upon what He reveals to you, it will become established in reality. By understanding, you will have a clear view of the furniture and how to decorate your home or whatever you've believed Him for. With this knowledge, you know how to diversify and implement the reality of those precious and pleasant things that will beautify your home.

COMMANDED TO LOVE

I DECREE AND DECLARE, "For God so loved the world, that he gave his only begotten Son, that whosoever believeth in him should not perish, but have everlasting life" (John 3:16).

PRACTICAL APPLICATION

According to 1 John 1:14, God is love, and because He is love, He gave all that He had for us, He paid the ransom for many, He gave His life on the cross that we may live according to John 3:16.

For God so loved the world that He gave His only begotten son (Jesus) that whosoever believe in Him should not perish but have everlasting life. That same love He had for the world He gave it to us to appropriate one toward another. Sometimes loving others is hard, but you can by faith; it's an act of your will. The Scripture says faith worketh by love, so it is imperative that we love as God commanded.

***

I DECREE AND DECLARE, "Charity suffereth long, and is kind; charity envieth not; charity vaunteth not itself, is not puff up, do not behave itself unseemly, seeketh not her own, is not easily provoked, thinketh no evil" (1 Corinthians 13:4-5).

33

PRACTICAL APPLICATION

Paul teaches us concerning our love walk, and he gives a description of what love is and how it operates; we have to appropriate it in our daily lives by faith and walk in it. When people mistreat you, that doesn't exempt you from walking in love. You have to choose and continue to walk in love; our love is being developed. Love produces long-suffering and kindness during challenging times. We are taught not to be self-seeking or self-center; it only leads to hurt and disappointments. We are not to provoke others to anger or think evil of people; we are to think the best of everyone.

***

I DECREE AND DECLARE, "There is no fear in love; but perfect love casteth our fear: because fear hath torment. He that feareth is not made perfect in love. (1 John 4:18).

PRACTICAL APPLICATION

I have learned fear is one of our emotions, and love is the opposite of fear, for fear has torment; I believe if we submit our fear to love, we will overcome the attacks it brings. The Father does not want His children tormented by anything. God had not given us a spirit of fear but power, love, and a sound mind. We must submit ourselves to God and resist the devil when he approaches us with fear. We must speak out of our mouths; I will not fear because Jesus loves me. And as we confess and proclaim His love, we will become more established in it until fear has to leave.

I DECREE AND DECLARE, "Be ye therefore followers of God, as dear children;" (Ephesians 5:1).

PRACTICAL APPLICATION

We are to follow God as dear children and walk in love; as a physical child tries to imitate his father or mother, we are to do the same toward our heavenly Father. As a matter of fact, it is a mandate. Not just in words but indeed also. We are called children of God and an heir of God, and joint heirs with Christ.

***

I DECREE AND DECLARE, "Love not the world, neither the things that are in the world. If any man love the world, the love of the Father is not in him. For all that is in the world, the lust of the flesh, lust of the eyes, and the pride of life is not of the Father, but is of the world" (1 John 2:15-16).

PRACTICAL APPLICATION

Love is the fruit of the Spirit that comes from God, and we are commanded to love one another as Christ has loved us and gave His life for us. First John 2:16-17 is talking about love, neither the world nor the things of the world. He is not talking about not loving people, but evil things people do. Remember Christ died for the sins of the world, and when He died, he gave us a way out of sin through His blood. When we exchange our sinful condition for His righteousness, we can come to Him and live a life of total victory and not defeat. We must be willing to spend time in the Word and allowing it to transform our lives in the way we think. You cannot live a victorious life with an old mindset or mentality. It has got to change, and that is a process. It starts with you. Now the three things that are mention are the lust of the flesh, lust of the eyes, and pride of life are merle appetite for the things of the world. When you desire those things more than God, they become your passion. He said in His word thou shalt have no other god before me.

JOY

I DECREE AND DECLARE, "For ye shall go out with joy, and be led forth with peace" (Isaiah 55:12).

PRACTICAL APPLICATION

You can always tell when God answers your prayer; there will be joy on the inside.

***

I DECREE AND DECLARE, "A merry heart doeth good like a medicine: but a broken spirit dried the bones" (Proverb17:22).

PRACTICAL APPLICATION

In my experience with the Lord, the joy of the Lord is our strength, and when you come into His presence, you can't help but rejoice because there is great power and an overwhelming of the anointing that rests upon and in you that causes a merry heart. As we spend quality time in His presence and meditate in His Word, we can become full of joy and possess a merry heart.

***

I DECREE AND DECLARE, " Let them shout for Joy, and be glad, that favour my righteous cause" (Psalm 35:27).

Thou Shalt Decree and Delcare

Practical Application

Let us give glory to God and rejoice and be glad, that favor His righteous cause, Christ Jesus is righteous, for He exchanges places with us on the cross when He became sin for us, making us righteous, and we are to shout it out, let the Lord be Magnified! which hath pleasure in the prosperity of His servant. God takes great pleasure and joy in blessing us with abundant life.

***

I DECREE AND DECLARE, "to appoint unto them that mourn in Zion, to give unto them beauty for ashes, the oil of Joy for mourning, the garment of praise for the spirit of heaviness; that they might be call a tree of righteousness, the planting of the Lord, that he might be glorified" (Isaiah 61:3).

Practical Application

God has taken our pains, shame, sorrows in Himself on the cross; what we call ashes is nothing but something that has been destroyed and burned up. And the spirit of joy for sadness, depression, and loneliness that comes from mourning. Being in His presence gives us hope and assurance that He's with us; and a covering of praise, which is glory and honor to His name.

***

I DECREE AND DECLARE, "Thou wilt shew me the path of life; in thy presence is fulness of joy; at thy right hand there are pleasures for evermore" (Psalm 16:11).

PRACTICAL APPLICATION

Life is a journey, and there is a path to travel, and in that path, we have choices to make, some good and others not so good. But whatever it may be, we are to choose life, not death. The Bible tells us in the presence of the Lord is the fullness of joy, and in that path is life eternal where the believer can come into His presence at any time and received from Him. When we speak of the right hand, we are always talking about the place of honor and power where we are seated with Him in heavenly places in Christ Jesus.

PEACE

I DECREE AND DECLARE, "Pray for peace of Jerusalem; they shall prosper that love thee. Peace be within thy walls, and prosperity within thy palaces" (Psalm 122:5, 6).

PRACTICAL APPLICATION

Always pray for the peace of Jerusalem; it is God's holy city where He put His name over 2,000 years ago. We are to pray for the peace of it because other nations have always tried to cease upon it. As we pray, the Bible said we shall be blessed, and serenity shall be inside our walls.

***

I DECREE AND DECLARE, "Thou will keep him in perfect peace, whose mind is stayed on thee because he trusted in thee" (Isaiah 26:3).

PRACTICAL APPLICATION

You might ask the question: is it possible to keep my mind stayed on God at all times? My answer is yes; as you walk alone and meditate upon His Word and pray them over yourself, God's Word will keep you in perfect peace. When thoughts of the enemy try to come and invade your peace, take authority over them with 2 Corinthians 10:4-6, casting down imagination and every high thing that goes against God's Word and replace it with the truth.

41

Thou Shalt Decree and Delcare

I DECREE AND DECLARE, "Therefore being Justified by faith; we have peace with God through my Lord Jesus Christ" (Roman 5:1).

Practical Application

The Scripture talks about being justified, as if we have done no wrong, Christ died for us, and we take it by faith in His finished work on the cross. Nothing that we have done, but it is all what He did for us.

***

I DECREE AND DECLARE, "Peace I leave with you, my peace I give unto you: not as the world giveth, give I unto you. Let not your heart be trouble, neither let it be afraid" (John 14:27).

Practical Application

God has a peace that transcends all understanding; I experience that about two weeks ago when my principal came into my workstation and told me, she was not going to sign my contract for next year. I had peace to come over me; I didn't get upset; I just kept doing my job, I asked why in a soft voice, and she gave me her reason. I said, God, I know you have a plan for me; you always do. God gives us a command to follow when trouble arises; we are not to let our hearts be trouble or afraid. We must watch the spirit of fear because it will approach us every time, but we don't have to receive it. We are to submit ourselves unto God, resist the devil, and he will flee from us.

***

I DECREE AND DECLARE: Be careful for nothing; but in everything by prayer and supplication with thanksgiving let your requests be made known unto God. And the peace of God, which passes all understanding, shall keep your hearts and minds through Christ Jesus (Philippians 4:6-7).

PRACTICAL APPLICATION
I have put this into practice in my life, and it works, I had been faced with a fiery trial, and my defense has always been standing on the Word and doing exactly what it says. I didn't become filled with anxiety or frustration; I prayed and gave God thanks, and let my request be made known unto God, lots of times I would write Him a letter, and afterward cast it upon Him by faith according to His Word in 1 Peter 5: 6-7 "Humble yourselves therefore under the mighty hand of God, that he may exalt you in due time; Casting all your care upon him; for he careth for you."

***

I DECREE AND DECLARE, "Who hath delivered us from the power of darkness, and hath translated us into the kingdom of his dear son" (Colossians 1:13).

PRACTICAL APPLICATION
Jesus died so that we could be set free from the power

of darkness (sin) and be translated into the kingdom of-
God's dear Son (light). Therefore, we are no more outsiders
or without a covenant, but a born-again citizen of faith in
God's kingdom.

***

I DECREE AND DECLARE, "Humble yourselves
therefore under the mighty hand of God, that he might exalt
you in due time: casting all your care upon him: for God
careth for you" (1 Peter 5:6-7).

PRACTICAL APPLICATION
God cares for each one of His children; no matter what
we are faced with, He is there to lighten our load. He tells
us to humble ourselves because there could be pried or
self-effort in our lives that is trying to compete with His
help, and God doesn't need any assistance. God will exalt
us in His timing as we let go and cast or throw our cares
upon Him.

***

I DECREE AND DECLARE, "for the kingdom of
God is not meat and drink; but righteousness, and peace
and joy in the Holy Ghost" (Roman 14:17).

PRACTICAL APPLICATION
The kingdom of God operates within me through the
presence of the Holy Spirit.

Sound Mind

I DECREE AND DECLARE, "For God has not given us the spirit of fear; but of power, and of love, and of a sound mind" (2 Timothy 1:7).

Practical Application
We know that fear comes from the enemy to hinder the believer's progress with the Lord. We must take our authority over fear binding its works over our lives in Jesus's name: replacing it with faith in God's Word. As we keep our minds stayed on Him, we will operate in soberness and soundness. In Isaiah 26:3, the Scripture says thou wilt keep him in perfect peace, whose mind is stayed on thee: because he trusted in thee.

***

I DECREE AND DECLARE, "I am not conformed to this world; but be ye transformed, by the renewing of your mind, that ye may prove what is that good, and acceptable, and perfect, will of God" (Roman 12:2).

Practical Application
We are not to fashion our lives and set our standard by the world way of living. We are to come out from among them and live as God has ordained. We bring our way of living in line with God's Word as we renew or make new our way of thinking.

THOU SHALT DECREE AND DELCARE

I DECREE AND DECLARE: For the weapons of our warfare are not carnal, but mighty through God to the pulling down of strong holds; casting down imagination, and every high thing that exalted itself against the knowledge of God, and bringing into captivity every thought to the obedience of Christ; and having in a readiness to revenge all disobedience, when your obedience is fulfilled (2 Corinthians 10:4-6).

PRACTICAL APPLICATION

As we study the Word and it becomes part of us, we know when thoughts come into our mind that is not of God, we are to take those thoughts captive and bring them into the obedience of Christ. We are to pull down images and cast down imagination every time a negative thought comes up in the mind that goes against His Word, take authority over it and pull it down and only say what the Scripture tells us. The mind is the battleground, and it is won by the Word of God.

***

I DECREE AND DECLARE, "Be sober, and vigilant, because your adversary the devil, as a roaring lion, walketh about, seeking whom he may devour" (1 Peter 5:8).

PRACTICAL APPLICATION

We must put on the mind of Christ because we have an enemy just waiting to take advantage of the believer who is not rooted in God's Word. We must be persistent and diligent in making a new mind according to God's Word.

***

I DECREE AND DECLARE: Blessed is the man that walketh not in the council of the ungodly, nor stand in the way of sinners, nor sitteth in the seat of the scornful. But his delight is in the law of the Lord and in his law doeth he meditates day and night. And he shall be like a tree planted by the rivers of water, that bringeth forth his fruit in his season; his leaf also shall not wither; and whatsoever he doeth shall prosper (Psalm 1:1-3**).**

PRACTICAL APPLICATION

The word blessed mean (happy) is the man that walketh not in the council (teaching) of the ungodly, nor stand in the way of sinners, nor seated in the seat of the scornful (bitter words) this man gives himself to the Word of God, and he ponders, mutter and speak the Word day and night to himself. The person who doeth these things shall be like a tree, which is not easily uprooted when it is planted by the water because it gets nutrient and nurture and become strong so that the winds of life come, it will prevail

***

I DECREE AND DECLARE, "Trust in the Lord with all thine heart; and lean not unto thine own understanding. In all thy ways acknowledge him, and he shall direct thy paths" (Proverb 3:5-6).

THOU SHALT DECREE AND DELCARE

PRACTICAL APPLICATION

To trust means to depend, put your confidence in, rely upon, and lay down in the Lord. We must believe the Word to the point of doing it. Don't depend upon your reasoning or your effort; acknowledge God in His Word, and He will give you a clear direction on what to do.

***

I DECREE AND DECLARE, "not by might, nor by power, but by my Spirit, says the Lord of hosts" (Zechariah 4:6).

PRACTICAL APPLICATION

Whatever mountain that is standing before you today can be level by the Spirit of God. In Zechariah 4:6, the Word of the Lord came unto Zerubbabel when he was facing his mountain, and the Lord intervened with a word to assure and secure him that the victory was his by the Spirit of God; just as it is ours when we are facing our mountain. In Mark 11:23-24, Jesus tells us to speak unto the mountain and command it to be removed and cast into the sea, if we wouldn't doubt in our heart, but believe those things which we said shall come to pass we can have whatsoever we said.

***

I DECREE AND DECLARE, "For as a man thinketh in his heart, so is he" (Proverb 23:7).

Practical Application

Our thought must be line up with the Word of God because whatever we think about goes into our hearts and comes out in our actions. So, we must make sure we are thinking positively and not negatively.

I AM PROTECTED

I DECREE AND DECLARE, "He that dwelleth in the secret place of the most High shall abide under the shadow of the almighty. I will say of the Lord, he is my refuge and my fortress: my God; in him will I trust" (Psalm 91:1-2).

PRACTICAL APPLICATION
Like baby chicken hides under the mother's wings for security and a hiding place, we as believers abide (dwell) under God Almighty, and we can say He is our protector, shelter, and hiding place, as we place all our trust and confidence in Him.

***

I DECREE AND DECLARE, "be not afraid of sudden fear, neither of the desolation of the wicked, when cometh. for the Lord shall be thy confidence and shall keep thy foot from being taken" (Proverb 3:25-26).

PRACTICAL APPLICATION
Proverb gives us a message of encouragement; we are not to be afraid of the attack of the enemy with sudden fear (easy to become afraid) because we put our confidence in Christ Jesus, and He is taking care of us.

***

THOU SHALT DECREE AND DELCARE

I DECREE AND DECLARE, "The Lord is my shepherd, and I shall not want" (Psalm 23:1).

PRACTICAL APPLICATION

A shepherd is one who takes care of the sheep. He loves, cares, and prepares a place of refuge for them. So, they have no need of a want

***

I DECREE AND DECLARE, "and the Lord shall deliver me from every evil work, and will preserve me unto his heavenly kingdom: to whom be glory for ever and ever Amen" (2 Timothy 4:18).

PRACTICAL APPLICATION

According to Colossians 1:13, we have been delivered from the power of darkness and translated into the kingdom of God's dear Son. Therefore we have the victory over every evil work because Christ completed it at the cross, and we must appropriate what He has done for us in the face of evil works.

***

I DECREE AND DECLARE, "whatever thou shall bind on earth shall be bound in heaven: and whatso thou shalt loose on earth shall be loosed in heaven" (Matthew 16:19).

I Am Protected

Practical Application

As the church, we have been given power and authority by Jesus Christ to bind and lose. Whatever we bind, bringing it to a complete naught in the Earth is bound in the heavenly atmosphere, and whatsoever we lose on Earth is the same as made free or let go.

***

I DECREE AND DECLARE, "Behold, I give unto you power to tread on that Jesus has given unto me power to tread on serpents and scorpions, and over all the power of the enemy: and nothing shall by any means hurt you" (Luke 10:19).

Practical Application

Jesus has given us power over all the works of the enemy; we don't have to be afraid of whatever he brings our way; because he is a defeated foe and has been put under our feet. Therefore, we walk in total victory and not defeat.

***

I DECREE AND DECLARE, "the angel of the Lord encamped around them that fear him, and delivered them" (Psalm 34:7).

Practical Application

You have been given authority to put your angels to work. Many people don't believe they are real and exist, and we have them. But I am a living witness they exist. I have seen angels, and they spoke to me in visions and dreams. We are surrounded by them to protect us and keep us safe if we believe the Word. They are to hearken to the voice of God's Word when we speak it.

THE ARMOR OF GOD

I DECREE AND DECLARE: Wherefore take unto you
the whole armor of God, that ye may be able to withstand
in the evil day, and having done all, to stand. Stand therefore, having your loins girt about with truth, and having on,
the breastplate of righteousness; and your feet shod with
the preparation of the Gospel of peace. Taking the shield
of faith, helmet of salvation, and the sword of the spirit,
which the word of God: Praying always with all prayers,
and supplication in the spirit, and watching thereunto with
all perseverance and supplication for all saints (Ephesians
6:14-18).

PRACTICAL APPLICATION

The armor of God is our essential garment for the
believers to put on and wear every day. We are covered and
protected by the Word of God daily. When trouble comes,
we are to take our stand in God's Word and stand until
something happens.

***

I DECREE AND DECLARE, "Submit yourselves
therefore to God. Resist the devil, and he will flee from
you" (James 4:7).

PRACTICAL APPLICATION

To submit to God means to humble yourself unto the

obedience of His Word and do it. To resist the devil means don't receive the lies, attacks, and distraction he brings your way. Take a stand against them by doing what the Word says to do.

***

I DECREE AND DECLARE, "that every plant, which the heavenly Father hath not planted, shall be rooted up" (Matthew 15:13).

PRACTICAL APPLICATION

As children of God, we have the authority to come against sickness, disease, mental distress, and symptom that comes against our body, spirit, and soul, plucking it up by the root and casting it out by faith in Jesus's name—speaking to it and telling it to get out of your body because it doesn't belong there. Jesus bored it all at Calvary cross, and we don't have to receive what the enemy tries to place on us.

***

I DECREE AND DECLARE, "God makes my storm calm, so that the waves thereof are still. Then are they glad because they be quiet; so, he bringeth them unto their desired haven" (Psalm 107:29).

PRACTICAL APPLICATION

We all have storms in our lives, one time or the other, and it is God that brings peace and calm to the storm. We

56

cannot master it in our own strength; we become stressed and burn out. Therefore, we turn everything over to Him, and He gives us joy and quietness, bringing us into a place of rest.

***

I DECREE AND DECLARE, "Be merciful unto me, O God, be merciful unto me: for my soul trusteth in thee; yea, in the shadow of thy wings will I make my refuge, until these calamities be overpast" (Psalm 57:1).

PRACTICAL APPLICATION

Thanks, God, for His mercy, they are new every morning, and His compassion fails not. Our soul (mind, will, emotional) trusts in Him, He is our shelter, and He keeps us steady until the storm is past.

***

I DECREE AND DECLARE, "A thousand shall fall at thy side, and ten thousand at thy right hand; but it shall not come nigh thee" (Psalm 91: 7).

PRACTICAL APPLICATION

In the midst of a situation that seems to be a threat to us, or just driving on the highways, we must remember that God has given us angels or ministering spirits to protect and keep us, even though we can't see them, they are with us, protecting and moving obstacle out of our way.

THOU SHALT DECREE AND DELCARE

I DECREE AND DECLARE, "We know that whosoever is born of God sinneth not; but he that is begotten of God keepeth himself, and that wicked one touches him not" (1 John 5:18).

PRACTICAL APPLICATION

We are born of God, and we don't have to sin; it is a decision on our part to sin or not, when we choose to do what right and hold to it, we keep ourselves, and the enemy cannot touch us. In one portion of Scripture, it tells us to shun the very presence of evil, meaning go from it, not toward it.

***

I DECREE AND DECLARE, "For God is not unrighteous to forget your work and labor of love, which ye have shewed toward his name, in that ye have ministered to the saints, and do minister" (Hebrews 6:10).

PRACTICAL APPLICATION

Sometimes I remind God of this very Scripture because sometimes, in your waiting on God, it seems He has forgotten you. But that is just my thought. He is not unrighteous to do that; He remembers all that we do in His name and some of the things we don't do. God never forgets, so know that whatever labor you have given and love you have shown will be on record with the Father.

THE ARMOR OF GOD

I DECREE AND DECLARE: "and this is the confidence that we have in him, that, if I ask anything according to his will, he heareth us: and if we know that he heareth us, whatever we ask, we know that we have the petition that we desire of him" (1 John 5:14-15).

PRACTICAL APPLICATION

When you asked God for something according to His Word, He hears you and will answer that prayer because it is asked in faith according to the Word. Remember His will is always His Word; whatever you see in the Scripture, you can ask for it. Our problem is, the time between asking and receiving, we have a tendency to waver and give up on Him when it doesn't come in a few days, or weeks, we lose our faith and start talking doubt and unbelief: which cancel the progress of the prayer you prayed, we just need to praise God for the answer until it comes.

PATIENCE

I DECREE AND DECLARE, "But let patient have her perfect work, that ye may be perfect and entire, wanting nothing" (James 1:4).

PRACTICAL APPLICATION
The word patient is not just waiting on God, but it is being consistent in the things of God. We must continue in His Word until He brings us into the place of the desired end results.

***

I DECREE AND DECLARE, "Rest in the Lord, and wait patiently for him; fret not thyself because of him who prospereth in his way, because of the man who bringeth wicked devices to pass" (Psalm 37:7).

PRACTICAL APPLICATION
We must choose to rest in His Word because our faith lies there: we must continue to do His will and wait on His promises to be manifest in our lives.

***

I DECREE AND DECLARE, "cast not away therefore your confidence, which hath great recompense of reward. For ye have need of patience, that, after you have done the will of God, ye might receive the promise" (Hebrews 10:35).

PRACTICAL APPLICATION

Don't fling or put aside your faith in God's Word, which will bring forth the reward or answer to what you have believed him for. After you have done His Word, employ patience which will undergird your faith until you received the promise.

***

I DECREE AND DECLARE, "But they that wait upon the Lord shall renew their strength; they shall mount up with wings as eagles; they shall run and not be weary, and they walk, and not faint" (Isaiah 40:31).

PRACTICAL APPLICATION

We are running the race of life, and sometimes we get weak and become weary, but the Scripture tells us that God will make new our strength like eagles as we minister unto Him, and gives us the grace to continue the race without being weary, and we can walk without giving out.

***

I DECREE AND DECLARE: "when thou passeth through the waters, I will be with thee: and through waters. I will be with thee; and through the rivers, they shall not overflow thee; When thou walkest through the fire, thou shall not be burned; neither shall the flame kindle upon thee. may kindle up against me, but I want get burned, for he is with me" (Isaiah 43:2).

PRACTICAL APPLICATION

You can be rest assured that you will go through trial and testing in this life, but be of good courage; you are not alone, God will always be with you, as you go through the waters and fires of life, know that you are protected and kept by the hand of God.

***

I DECREE AND DECLARE, "I waited patiently for the Lord; and he inclined unto me, and heard my cry" (Psalm 40:1).

PRACTICAL APPLICATION

Waiting on God will develop your endurance and help you grow in confidence and assurance in Him.

WEALTHY AND BLESSED

I DECREE AND DECLARE, "thou hast caused men to ride over our heads; we went through fire and through water: but thou have brought us out into a wealthy place" (Psalm 66:12).

PRACTICAL APPLICATION

This is a song of praise unto God, for carrying them through tough times, men rode over their heads, but they did not prevail, and now he has brought them into a rich and flourishing place.

***

I DECREE AND DECLARE, "So then they which be of faith, are blessed with faithful Abraham" (Galatians 3:9).

PRACTICAL APPLICATION

Abraham was called the Father of faith because he believed God in the face of all odds; he walked and talked with God, and whatever he was commanded to do, he did it. That same example of faith is what we are called upon to do as children of God, to walk by faith and not by sight.

THOU SHALT DECREE AND DELCARE

I DECREE AND DECLARE, "Blessed be the God and Father of our Lord Jesus Christ who have blessed us with all spiritual blessings in heavenly *places* in Christ Jesus" (Ephesians 1; 3).

PRACTICAL APPLICATION
Know that you are blessed, and you have all the privileges of Jesus Christ because we are children of the Father and heirs of God and joint-heirs with Christ.

***

I DECREE AND DECLARE, " Blessed be the Lord, who daily loadeth us with benefits, even the God of our Salvation" (Psalm 68:19).

PRACTICAL APPLICATION
We are the Lord's prized possession, and He has loaded and equipped us with whatever we need for our daily supply.

***

I DECREE AND DECLARE, "His seed shall be mighty upon the earth, the generation of the upright shall be blessed" (Psalm 112:2).

PRACTICAL APPLICATION
Our seeds are our offspring, and they shall be blessed

and mighty upon Earth; of the upright generation.

***

I DECREE AND DECLARE, "blessed is the man that feareth the Lord, him, that delighted greatly in his Commandments" (Psalm112:1).

PRACTICAL APPLICATION
We are blessed by the Lord because we honor and reference Him and give ourselves to His word daily.

***

I DECREE AND DECLARE, "Delight thyself also in the Lord; and he shall give thee desires of thine heart" (Psalm 37:4).

PRACTICAL APPLICATION
The Bible says as we delight ourselves in the Word to do it, God gives us our heart desires, whatever they may be, as long as it is in line with His Word. Many times He places desires in our hearts to fulfill His plans for our lives. Remember, as parents, we don't give our children everything they want because it is unhealthy. So likewise, with the Father, He is not going to give us everything we want; but if we commit our ways and heart desires unto Him, He will bring them to pass.

GRACE AND FINANCES

I DECREE AND DECLARE, "The Spirit himself beareth witness with our spirit that we are the children of God" (Roman 8:16).

PRACTICAL APPLICATION

Grace is God's unmerited favor, which He bestowed upon us through His Son Jesus Christ. He gave it freely and willingly to us; we didn't deserve it. When He went back to the Father, He sent back the comforter, which is the Holy Spirit to teach, lead and guide us into all truth: and He is our witness that we are children of God.

***

I DECREE AND DECLARE, "grace and peace is multiple unto me through the knowledge of God and of Jesus our Lord" (2 Peter 1:2).

PRACTICAL APPLICATION

As we receive the knowledge or instruction in God's Word, grace and peace are accumulated over and over again to us through the revelation of Jesus Christ.

***

I DECREE AND DECLARE, "For thou, Lord. will bless the righteous with favor, and will compass him as with a shield" (Psalm 5:12).

PRACTICAL APPLICATION
The believers are the righteousness of God in Christ
Jesus, and He pours out His favor upon us through His love
and encircles us with His favor and protected armor.

***

I DECREE AND DECLARE, "But the Lord was with
Joseph. And shewed him mercy and gave him mercy, and
gave him favor in the sight of the keeper of the prisoners"
(Genesis 39:21).

PRACTICAL APPLICATION
We have the same privileges as Joseph did when he
walks in the midst of the people of God and others with
favor and mercy. We are God's children, and He loves us
equally and has given us favor and mercy also.

***

I DECREE AND DECLARE, "the Lord shall open
unto me his good treasure, the heaven to give me rain in my
land in its season, and to bless all the works of thine hand;
and thou shalt lend unto nation and not borrow" (Deuteronomy 28:12).

PRACTICAL APPLICATION
The Lord has ordained for His children to walk in

more than enough, but it is always through His grace that He blesses us and causes us to prosper. There are different seasons in our lives that He pours out His rain and bless the works of our hands, making us suppliers to others.

***

I DECREE AND DECLARE, "the Lord Shall make thee the head, and not the tail; thou shall be above only, and thou shalt not beneath; which I command thee this day to observe and do them" (Deuteronomy 28:13).

PRACTICAL APPLICATION

We have been made the head of all things and not the tail because of our position in Christ and what He has done for us. In obedience to His Word, He blesses us as we keep His saying and do His commands. As a child of God, I choose to hearken and be a doer of His Word.

***

I DECREE AND DECLARE, "House and riches are the inheritance of the fathers: and a prudent wife is from the Lord" (Proverb 19:14).

PRACTICAL APPLICATION

This is a promise of God to the believer that believes His Word and does accordingly, and a wife of understanding is from the Lord.

71

THOU SHALT DECREE AND DELCARE

I DECREE AND DECLARE, "And I will give thee the treasures of darkness, and hidden riches of secret places, that thou mayest know that I, the Lord which calls thee by thy name, am the God of Israel" (Isaiah 45:3).

PRACTICAL APPLICATION
God will give unto His children those deposits of darkness and hidden riches of unknown places which ungodly men think are kept secret.

***

I DECREE AND DECLARE, "But thou shalt remember the Lord thou God: for it is he that giveth thee power to get wealth, that he may establish his covenant which he sware unto thy fathers, as it is this day" (Deuteronomy 8:18).

PRACTICAL APPLICATION
As God gives us wealth, we are to help get the Gospel out to other countries and nations with our giving. There are still people who have not heard the Gospel, and it has to be preached all over the world before Christ comes back for His church.

***

I DECREE AND DECLARE, "every place where on the sole of your feet shall tread shall me yours" (Deuteronomy 11:24).

PRACTICAL APPLICATION

Just as Caleb obeyed the Word of the Lord, decreeing that wherever he placed his feet shall be his, we are to do the same and take possession of whatever God has given unto us through His Word. It does not come without courage and a fight of faith; we must press into it and take ownership. God has spoken, and His words are true; we must rise up and know that He is with us as He was with the children of Israel.

***

I DECREE AND DECLARE, "Bring ye all the tithes into the storehouse, that there may be meat in mine house, and proves me now herewith, saith the Lord of hosts, If I will not open you the windows of heaven and pour you out a blessing, that there shall not be room enough to receive it" (Malachi 3:10).

PRACTICAL APPLICATION

Living a life of a tither is a great blessing to me; I look forward to bringing my tithe and offering and giving them to the Lord. He has blessed me in so many ways when I was sick. I stood on the promises of a tither, with my family, calling back to God His Word. He promises to rebuke the devourer for our sake so that my ground would be blessed. God is a man of His word, we sometimes get impatient with Him because we want things now, and sometimes we really need the turnaround, but He works in His own time and is never late.

***

I DECREE AND DECLARE, "Give and it shall be given unto you: good measure, press down and shaken together and running over, shall men give into your bosom. For with the same measure that ye mete withal, it shall be measured to you again (Luke 6:38).

Practical Application

The Bible tells us to give in obedience; we obey, we don't give with an attitude of necessity, but as we give it is given unto us, to the full and overflow, men give into our bosom. Whatever we give it comes back to us in abudance

I WALK IN DOMINION

I DECREE AND DECLARE, "God blessed them, and God said unto them. Be fruitful and multiply, and replenish the earth. And subdue it and have dominion over the fish of the sea, over the fowl of the air, and over every living thing that moveth upon earth" (Genesis 1:28).

PRACTICAL APPLICATION

He ordained man to walk in dominion and authority over everything He made and put on Earth. He made man to triumph and have victories over every living and creeping thing and told Him to multiply and subdue and replenish the Earth. We are to walk in what he has given us.

***

I DECREE AND DECLARE, "with open face beholding as in a glass the glory of the Lord, are changed into the same image from glory to glory even as by the Spirit of the Lord" (2 Corinthians 3:18).

PRACTICAL APPLICATION

As we come into the presence of God and experience His glorious power, He brings forth an illumination in our lives. Sometimes, we can't see it, but others can. We are to change from glory to glory as a bright light that shineth in darkness.

THOU SHALT DECREE AND DELCARE

I DECREE AND DECLARE, "that Jesus is the brightness of his glory, and the express image of his person and upholding all things by the word of his power" (Hebrews 1:3).

PRACTICAL APPLICATION

Put the word to work in your life. God's Word carries power and changes lives permanently. The Word of God healed the body and makes it alive, cast out demons. His Word is supernatural and does supernatural things.

***

I DECREE AND DECLARE, "I say unto you, whatsoever I bind on earth shall be bound in heaven and whatsoever ye shall loose on earth shall be loosed in heaven" (Matthew 18:18).

PRACTICAL APPLICATION

You have been given the power to capture anything on Earth that comes against you and to free anything on Earth that will bless you.

***

I DECREE AND DECLARE, "If two of us shall touch and agree on earth as touching anything, it shall be done for them of my Father which is in heaven" (Matthew 18:19).

PRACTICAL APPLICATION

When you apply the power of agreement in prayer, things happen. Prayers are answered, and situations are turned around. As we touch and agree and stand on the spoken word, it will come to pass in the believer's life.

***

I DECREE AND DECLARE, "Behold I give unto you power to tread on serpents and scorpions and over all the power of the enemy and nothing shall by any means hurt you" (Luke 10:19).

PRACTICAL APPLICATION

I use to be afraid of dreams about serpents, but I realize they were attacks of the enemy, and we have been given authority over all the works of the enemy, and Jesus said, nothing by any means shall hurt us.

***

I DECREE AND DECLARE, "Go ye therefore and teach all nations baptizing them in the name of the Father, and of the son and of the Holy Ghost, teaching them to observe all thing whatsoever he commanded you and low he's with me always even to the end of the world" (Matthew 28:19-20).

PRACTICAL APPLICATION

Authority has been given to the church by Jesus Christ, and as we go, we are to carry the gospel to all nations, teach and baptizing them in the name of the Father, Son, and Holy Ghost. We are to observe (pay attention to do) all that He gives instruction to do, and He is with us always to the end of the world.

My Inheritance

I DECREE AND DECLARE, "as if children, then heir; heirs of God, and joint-heirs with Christ; if so be That we suffer with him, that we may be also glorified together" (Roman 8:17).

Practical Application

Because of Jesus' death, burial, and resurrection, He became the mediator of the New Testament, causing us to be heir of God and joint-heirs with Christ. Therefore, being like Him and identifying with His death and resurrection, we to must suffer with Him and be glorified with Him

***

I DECREE AND DECLARE, "now unto him that is able to do exceedingly abundantly above all that we ask or think, according to the power that worketh in us" (Ephesians 3:20).

Practical Application

There are times in our lives circumstances seem bigger and overwhelming to us, but we must remember that God is all-powerful within us, and He can exceed what we ask or think of Him, according to the Holy Spirit that worked in us.

THOU SHALT DECREE AND DELCARE

I DECREE AND DECLARE, "The Lord knoweth the days of the upright; and their inheritance shall be forever" (Psalm 37:18).

PRACTICAL APPLICATION

God has numbered our days, and our inheritance is in His hand, and He will bring it to pass in His own time because of His Word.

ABOUT THE AUTHOR

I was born in Marquez, Texas, attended the Buffalo Bennet Elementary School in Buffalo, Texas, and the George Washington Carver school until 1968 and graduated from Leon High School in 1972. Attended Navarro Jr. College for one year and got married the next and started a family. Later on in life, God saved me and gave me a new life in Him. I became a member of the Mount Horeb Baptist church under the leadership of late C. O. Smith. I am a God-fearing woman, called by God as a messenger for Him in 1996. A prayer warrior and songster to the body of Christ, I demonstrate God's love toward others as I come in contact with them. Married for forty-seven years to Henry A. Payne, minister and former pastor, and have two beautiful children and two handsome grandsons. I have seven living siblings and one deceased brother and a living mother who is ninety-four years old. I have been blessed beyond measure; God has graced me in many ways with hidden talent that He is now uncovering in this hour of my life.

I am a co-founder of Living by Faith ministries, which started as a church with about fifty members, until the Lord told my husband that we were to move to Denton, TX to start a new church there. We remain there for seven years and move back to Lewisville Texas, where I went back to school and attended North Central Texas College and received my Associate degree. I had the privilege of being in a leadership position as pastor wife, a teacher of the young adult group call the willing workers, and a Senior mission group. I have spoken at various churches and conferences.

This book was written to inform readers that with God, all things are possible to him that believes. As we become established in His Word, we will grow and superabound in faith.

My family and I are now attending (EMIC) Eagle Mountain International church in Newark, Texas We have been members for twelve years. We love our pastor and wife and members.

I PRAY THAT
GOD WILL BLESS YOU AND KEEP YOU.
THE LORD MAKES HIS FACE SHINE
UPON YOU, AND BE GRACIOUS UNTO
YOU; THE LORD WILL LIFT UP HIS
COUNTENANCE UPON YOU AND
GIVE YOU PEACE. AMEN!

CPSIA information can be obtained
at www.ICGtesting.com
Printed in the USA
BVHW041706080721
611459BV00015B/1113

9 781637 694367